A Mega Moti...
Crash Course On God's Heart...

God's Great

Ambition

by *Dan & Dave Davidson &*
George Verwer

God's Great Ambition

by Dan & Dave Davidson & George Verwer

brought to you by DailyMissions.com

© 2001 ThinkWow - Inspire Books
& GeorgeVerwer.com

ISBN 0-9636177-7-X

cover design & layout by Dave Davidson & Marji Guyler

photos by Dave Davidson & Corell stock photos,
author pictures by Joan Davidson & Ginger Brick

printed in Canada by VISTAinfo Canada Inc.

pages numbers intentionally left out to encourage
the following of scriptures in order of the bible

For complete Biliography please visit
GodsGreatAmbition.com

Foreword

This unique book of spiritual dynamite needs to be read and prayed over by people around the globe. I have known Dave and Joan Davidson for many years and had the privilege of working together with them in Europe in the amazing combination ministry of hospitality and mission mobilization. They are people who are putting into practice the message that they have put into this very special book.

I want to urge you to buy at least 10 copies and become a distributor of what many would consider to be one of the most needed exhortations or messages needed by God's people.

I believe the Holy Spirit can use these words, some of them right from the Scriptures to motivate thousands into action, reality and world missions.

Let's remember James 1:22 and make sure that we are not just hearers but doers of the Word. Why not read also Isaiah 6:8 and then pray that prayer in verse, 'Here am I send me'.

George Verwer

WARNING: contents may eternally effect change in your life and others.

What is your calling, your purpose, and your mission? Jesus revealed His mission in the Great Commission. God doesn't have ambition like man's desires t aspire success. He does however reveal His will that none should perish.

Let's align our lives with the ambition God offers us in sharing the gospel. God's Great Ambition is that you be a vessel in fulfilling His promise. God's Grea Ambition for you is an abundant life following, trusting and serving Him.

You may not know it yet, but perhaps the greatest challenge of your life is before you now. The pages that follow are a crash course on God's heart, designed encourage and challenge the Christian to have increased awareness, action and ownership in the Great Commission. Get ready to pray, give, go, and follow.

A chronological journey from God's word is blended with timely testimonie An urgent missionary call is set forth. Confident, convicting and comforting word melt church pews into starting blocks of service in the race of faith. It's time to jur from the bleachers and dash into eternity. There's no time for sugar coating. Nap time is not promoted. There's only time for God's compassionate truth.

With conviction from the Holy Spirit let these challenges question, confront and let them dare. Some may mistake the devil's line that you can't be involved in the missionary journey. But, God has a part for everyone in His mission plan. He so faithful, so powerful, so patient, so purposeful - He will empower you.

You need to be willing to get your feet wet and walk with Him. So dare to answer the call to action. Dare to make a world of difference. Dare to make your great ambition God's Great Commission.   *Dan & Dave Davidson*

The visionary who is serving God
ceases to live for personal ambition,
but rather for God's ambitions.

George Barna

LIFE IS A VAPOR

You can change your destiny. You can change your fate. If there's something you're becoming that you didn't want to be... Turn around before it's too late. Turn around before it's too late. The things that were gained I now count them as lost. The things that were lost, now as gain. The person I was I decided to toss, that's why I'll never again be the same, never again be the same. So you're living in the city or is it living in you? Cause you let it take you under, says there's nothing you can do. Now the world has all its problems, but you let it rob you of your hope. You say what's the use in trying, with all the pain I just can't cope. But my life is a vapor and I won't let it waste away just step back into the fire you could live and breath it today. Mediocrity, complacency get away from me you're not my friends anymore. It gets harder everyday, but then I hear my Fath say don't worry "I'm keeping the score. Don't worry I'm keeping the score." Not gonna take it anymore, not gonna settle for less, not gonna l down on the floor, I want to do my best. I'm gonna be just who I need to be, not be just what I am and as long as I have this voice to speak I'm gonna say just what I can.

Robert Rottet - listen to the song at PoetTree.com

World Missions

was on God's mind from the beginning.

"I will make you into a great nation and I will bless you;
I will make your name great, and you will be a blessing.
I will bless those who bless you, and whoever curses you I will
curse; and all peoples on earth will be blessed through you."

Genesis 12:2,3

**There is a living God. He has spoken His word.
He means just what he says, and will do
all that he has promised.**

J. Hudson Taylor

A ship in harbor is safe, but
that is not what ships are built for.

William Shedd

The future is as bright as the promise of God.

William Carey

God's main intention in human history is to reunite himself
with a world that is estranged by sin. All that he is doing in space
and time is an effort to further that desire. From the first verses of
Genesis to the last verses of Revelation, his intention is articulated and
illustrated. The wonder of it all is that he wants to accomplish this
mission through the faithfulness of people like you and me.

John M. Criswell

*(hypothetical prayer from the lost
if they even knew what to pray)*

URGENT! URGENT!

Send workers; Send bibles; Save my soul; Save my people;
Send a love revival. We are hoping. We are choking.
We are going to hell. Give up your small ambitions.
Show us eternal living, I need to know about Jesus.
Don't you see I need to believe. Don't let me be
another eternal statistic.

Dave Davidson

We are not only called to evangelize the world,
but we are called to build the kingdom everywhere.
This means that your work matters to God.

George Verwer

We have missionaries coming back from the fields and not able to go back, unable to find dynamic, live, cutting edge, mega motivated, Acts 13 sending churches. We must bring this into the equation. We must understand what is to release finance through prayer and faith and put the ministry of sending on an absolute equal level with the ministry of going. It will be a battle all the way.

George Verwer

The gates of heaven are not closed for the Communists. Neither is the light quenched for them. They can repent like everyone else. And we must call them to response. Only love can change the communist and the terrorist.

Richard Wurmbrand

Of all the prophets, Jesus alone was resurrected from the dead, and he remains our living Mediator forever. I gave my life into His hands. For me, life is an opportunity to serve Him and death is the privilege of getting to be with Him.

Medi Dibaj

Exodus 6:6 ... I will **redeem** you with an outstretched arm and with mighty acts of judgment. *Exodus 15:13* **In your unfailing love** you will lead the people you have redeemed. In your strength you will guide them to your holy dwelling.

If you found a cure for cancer it would be

inconceivable

to hide it from the rest of mankind. How much more inconceivable to keep silent the cure from the eternal wages of death.

Dave Davidson

**No one understands Scripture
unless it is brought home to him,
that is, unless he experiences it.**

Martin Luther

IT'S ESTIMATED THAT HUNDREDS
OF PEOPLE SHARE THE SAME BIBLE IN
CHINA'S UNDERGROUND CHURCH.

*...I carried you on eagles' wings
and brought you to myself.*
Now if you obey me fully and keep my
covenant, then out of all nations you
will be my treasured possession...

Exodus 19:4,5

In our
lifetime,
wouldn't it be sad
if we
spent
more

TIME

washing dishes or swatting flies or
mowing the yard or watching sitcoms...
than praying for world missions!

Dave Davidson

For the LORD your God is a
consuming fire, a jealous God.
Deuteronomy 4:24

Know therefore
that the Lord your God **is** God;
he **is** the faithful God, keeping his covenant
of love to a thousand generations of those
who love him and keep his commands.

Deuteronomy 7:9

Be strong
and courageous.

Do not be terrified; do not be discouraged,
for the Lord your God will be with you wherever you go.

Joshua 1:8,9

**(a) Pray (b) Give (c) Go (d) Follow
answer - (e) all the above**

Dan Davidson

But if serving the Lord seems undesirable to you,
then *choose* for yourselves this day whom you will serve...

... But as for me and my household, we will serve the LORD.
Joshua 24:15

Your perspective of yourself will determine the possibilities you pursue.

Mike Evans

As a true believer you are God's child. Jesus is within you.
To you, to everyone, he is saying, 'I want to be your Lord,
I want to be the king of your life. I want to control your
time, your talents, your money, your holidays, your
work, your marriage. Come to me, to the foot of
the cross, and make me Lord of your life.

George Verwer

Visionaries

are never willing to shelve God's vision simply
because the resources appear to be unavailable...
One of the most remarkable truths about vision is
that when the vision is implemented, the result is
creating, rather than consuming resources.

George Barna

If only we could see the value of one soul like God does.

George Verwer

For the **sake** of his great name
the LORD will *not* reject his people,
because the LORD was *pleased* to make you his *own*.
1 Samuel 12:22

From the stories
of others who have become

involved

in mission work, we learn that the initial inner
urgings often seem very subtle, hard to discern.
In fact, for most of us, the message really doesn't
become clear until we act. It is the process of taking
action in response to the Holy Spirit's urging
that often provides the real clarity. Without
responding, you'll probably never know.

Tetsunao Yamamori

**For the eyes of the Lord range
throughout the earth to strengthen
those whose hearts are fully
committed to him.**

2 Chronicles 16:9

Everyone one of us can be some sort of a
philanthropist.

Dave Davidson

The Great Commission is more than a call for you
or me to leave where we are and go somewhere else.
There is of course a great need for people to go, but
there is a greater need for each of us to take up our own
responsibility as part of the church's response to the
Great Commission; to be personally involved in
it whatever our particular role may be.

George Verwer

Who will listen to what you say?
The *share* of the man
who stayed with the supplies
is to be the *same* as that of him
who went down to the battle.
All will share alike.

1 Samuel 30:24

Possessions are not given that we may
rely on them and glory in them but that
we may use and enjoy them and share
them with others... Our possessions
should be in our hands, not in our hearts.

Martin Luther

Prayer is one of the great altars
where God makes true men and women.

George Verwer

...Intercede

with the LORD your God and pray for me...

1 Kings 13:6

What we see depends mainly on what we look for.

John Lubbock

Develop the discipline of not giving up or in.

Cyrano De Words-u-lac

God, grant me the

serenity

to accept people that drive me crazy;
the courage to up and get going; and the
wisdom to know you love the bananas
out of me even when I screw things up.

Hugh Myrrh

Declare his glory among the nations,
his marvelous deeds among all peoples.
1 Chronicles 16:24

Don't measure yourself by what you have accomplished,
but by if God's will is being accomplished through you.

Dan Davidson

**No one has the right
to hear the gospel twice,
while there remains someone
who has not heard it once.**

Oswald J. Smith

Get in the action whatever the cost,
nothing can equal the worth of the lost.
Shoulder to shoulder, hand to the plow
today is the day and the right time is now.

Bob Hartman

God loves everything about you and He loves you still.

A. W. Tozer

I never knew a child of God
bankrupted by his benevolence.
What we keep we may lose, but what
we give to Christ we are sure to keep.

Theodore L. Cuyler

No one can out-give God.

George Verwer

Maybe a change of attitude
would help change our world vision.
While brothers and sisters perish you could make
a world of difference.

Dave Davidson

I know
    that you
        can do
            all things;
no plan
    of yours
        can be
            thwarted.

J o b 42:2

After failure, do you sometimes feel you have missed plan A for your life? If you do, then thank God for His sovereignty and the reality of Romans 8:28: We know that all things work together for good for those who love God, who are called according to his purpose. Plan B or C can be just as great as plan A. You may think that you have made a lot of mistakes and taken a lot of wrong turnings in your life. Perhaps you feel you are on plan F or G. I say, 'Praise God for a big alphabet' and press on! No matter how many heartbreaks, disappointments and difficulties there may be, we need to keep a positive, grace-awakened attitude and keep moving forward in our response to the call of Jesus to be His witnesses throughout the world.

George Verwer

Scripture is clear. Our responsibilities do not end with Jerusalem.

George Verwer

Your mission, if you decide to accept it,
is an exciting, adventurous abundant life with
almighty God as your very own personal guide in
following His plan, on His terms, with His power.

Dave Davidson

1 IN *5* PEOPLE ARE MALNOURISHED

Most people buy things they don't need with money they don't have to impress people they don't like.

anonymous

If I could live my life again...
I would give more to the poor.

Cyrano De Words-u-lac

We should pray about missions until
it becomes a priority! We may not personally
be able to take the good news abroad, but we can all
pray in such a way that regions abroad are affected...

Prayer needs no passport,

visa or work permit. There is no such thing as a
'closed country' as far as prayer is concerned... Much
of the history of mission could be written in terms of
God moving in response to persistent prayer.

Stephen Gaukroger

Ask of Me,

and I will make the nations your inheritance,
the ends of the earth your possession.

Psalm 2:8

There are no closed doors to the gospel,
provided that, once you go through the door,
you don't care whether or not you come back out.

Brother Andrew

Do you realize that you and
I are God's gift to the world?

Josh McDowell

Let us commit ourselves to the joyful discipline
of honoring Jesus Christ by our actions.

Bill Bright

I am sure that God is already using many of you more than you realize. Be aware of the subtleties of putting yourself down in an unbiblical way, just as I am sure you would beware of allowing yourself to be puffed up. Be aware that God is doing great things in the world today. He is working through older churches, newer churches, older agencies and newer agencies in an exciting way.

George Verwer

This is your chance.

Live your life as a big thank you to God,
by storing up rewards to place at
the feet of Jesus in heaven.

Dave Davidson

Serve the LORD with fear and rejoice with trembling.

Therefore I will praise you among the nations, O LORD; I will sing praises to your name.

Psalms 2:11; 18:49

There are many of us that are willing to do great things for the Lord, but few of us are willing to do little things.

D. L. Moody

Changes in my own heart occur as I work to see change in others. For me, missions teaches me that it's never all about me.

Jill Hekman

pproximately

25% of
SCRIPTURE
distribution.

s directed toward the
east-evangelized world

<u>MISSION CONDITION:</u>
For every unreached people group there are over
400 evangelical churches & over 40,000 believers.

Every day that passes is
one day closer to Christ's return.

Dan Davidson

But the plans of the LORD stand firm forever,
the purposes of his heart through all generations.
Blessed is the nation whose God is the LORD,
the people he chose for his inheritance.
Psalms 33:10,11

God has not called me to be successful;
he has called me to be faithful.

Mother Teresa

The crucial thing is to be a

partner in missions

wherever you are.

Stephen Gaukoger

What an honor it is to participate in any part of delivering
the greatest hope of all mankind... The good news of Jesus.

Dave Davidson

The church has many organizers,
but few agonizers.

Leonard Ravenhill

There is no substitute

for daily denying self and taking up the cross,
regardless of your circumstances… Created as we are
in the image of God, He has given us a free will and we
are fully responsible for making the right decisions and
taking the right steps on a moment-by-moment basis.

George Verwer

"Be still, and **know** that **I am God**;
I will be exalted among the nations,
I will be exalted in the earth."

Psalms 46:10

Psalm 86:11

Teach me your way, O LORD,
and I will walk in your truth;
give me an *undivided* heart,
that I may fear your name.

Seeking to perpetuate one's name
on earth is like writing on the sand
by the seashore; to be perpetual
it must be written on the
eternal shores.

D. L. Moody

THE GREAT SIN OF THE WORLD
IS NOT THAT THE HUMAN RACE
HAS FAILED TO WORK FOR GOD
SO AS TO *INCREASE* HIS GLORY,
BUT THAT WE HAVE FAILED TO

DELIGHT IN GOD

SO AS TO *REFLECT* HIS GLORY.
**FOR GOD'S GLORY IS MOST
REFLECTED IN US WHEN WE
ARE MOST DELIGHTED IN HIM.**

John Piper

Be exalted, O God, above
the heavens, and let your
glory be over all the earth.
Psalms 108:5

The gospel **is only good news** if it arrives in time.

Carl F. H. Henry

**Like cold water to a weary soul
is good news from a distant land.**

Proverbs 25:25

When the
world sees millions of

"retired" Christians

pouring out the last drops of
their lives with *joy* for the sake
of the unreached peoples and
with a view toward heaven,
then the supremacy of God will *shine*.
He does not *shine* as brightly
in the posh, leisure-soaked luxury condos
on the outer rigs of our cities.

John Piper

Attempt
great things for God.
Expect
great things from God.

William Carey

Where there is no vision
the people perish.

Proverbs 29:18 (NKJV)

He has made
everything beautiful in its time.

He has also set

eternity

in the hearts of men;

yet they cannot fathom what God has done from beginning to end.
I know that everything God does will endure forever;
nothing can be added to it and nothing taken from it.

God does it so that men will revere him.

Ecclesiates 3:11,14

I HEAR THE *ROAR* OF MY REBELLION,
AND IT DRIVES ME TO MY KNEES
AS I WEIGH MY STRONG DESIRE TO BE

S U C C E S S F U L

AGAINST WHAT I BELIEVE
I'VE HEARD THE COMMANDS, READ CHAPTER AND VERSE
BUT I CAN'T WASH MY HANDS FROM THE *BLOOD OF* THE CURSED

Bill Drake

Now all has been heard; here is the
conclusion of the matter:
Fear God and keep his commandments,
for this is the whole duty of man.
Ecclesiates 12:13

... "whom shall I send? And who will go for us?"
And I said, "Here I am. Send me!"

Isaiah 6:8

"...You are my witnesses,"
declares the LORD "that I am God..."

Isaiah 43:12

The Spirit of the Sovereign Lord is on me, because the LORD has anointed me
to preach good news to the poor. He has sent me to bind up the brokenhearted,
to proclaim freedom for the captives and release from darkness for the prisoners..
Isaiah 61:1

For Zion's sake I will not keep silent, for Jerusalem's sake
I will not remain quiet, till her righteousness shines out
like the dawn, her salvation like a blazing torch.
Isaiah 62:1

"For I know the plans I have for you," declares the LORD, "plans to prosper and not harm you, plans to give you hope and a future."

Jeremiah 29:11

'Call to me and I will answer you and tell you great and unsearchable things which you do not know.'

Jeremiah 33:3

The greatest missions movement in history is taking place right now. **You'd have to be dumb to think this stuff isn't exciting!**

George Verwer

For I take no pleasure in the death of anyone, declares the Sovereign Lord. Repent and live!

Ezekiel 18:32

I looked for a man
among them who would stand before me in the gap...

Ezekiel 22:30

He rescues and he saves...

Daniel 6:27

GIVE UP
YOUR SMALL AMBITIONS

J. Hudson Taylor & Francis Xavier

Multitudes, multitudes in the valley of decision!
For the day of the Lord is near in the valley of decision.

Joel 3:14

Fanatic:

A person who's enthusiastic about something in which you have no interest.

Albert J. Nimeth

"But I don't have any special talents or abilities that would qualify me to be a missionary." Then you're just the person God is looking for.

Keith Green

Those who cling to worthless idols forfeit the grace that could be theirs. But I, with a song of thanksgiving, will sacrifice to you. What I have vowed I will make good. Salvation comes from the Lord.

Jonah 2:8,9

The Great Commission is
not an option
to be considered, it is a command to be obeyed.

J. Hudson Taylor

So many suffer so much while so few sacrifice so little.

Bob Pierce

*...Should I not be concerned
about that great city.*

Jonah 4:11

But as for me, I am filled
with power, with the Spirit of the Lord.

Micah 3:8

Look at the nations and watch- and
be utterly amazed.

For I am going to do something in your days that
you would not believe, even if you were told.

Habakkuk 1:5

The Lord your God is with you, he is mighty to save.
He will take great delight in you, he will quiet you
with his love, he will rejoice over you with singing.

Zephaniah 3:17

I believe the reason many Christians are so dull and lifeless in their faith is because they are not

in the battle,

not using their weapons, not advancing

against the enemy.

George Verwer

'Not by might nor by power, but my Spirit,' says the LORD Almighty.

Zechariah 4:7

God wants to have a relationship
with all his children in all his nations.
We must **introduce** them to Him.

Dan Ayres

"My name will be great among the
nations, from the rising to the setting sun."
Malachi 1:11

The evangelistic harvest is always urgent.
The destiny of men and of nations
is always being decided.

Billy Graham

What we are is God's gift to us. What we become is our gift to God.

Louis Nizer

God made you as you are in order to use you as He planned.

S.C. McAuley

"Bring the whole tithe into the storehouse, that there may be food in my house. Test me in this," says the Lord Almighty, "and see if I will not throw open the flood gates of heaven and pour out so much blessing that you will not have room enough for it."

Malachi 3:10

I must surrender my fascination with myself to a more worthy preoccupation with the character and purposes of God. I am not the point. He is. I exist for him. He does not exist for me.

Larry Crabb

Take ownership

in the Great Commission like a stockholder does in a company, and in heaven you'll be a rich spiritual millionaire.

George Verwer

Got to the gates of heaven... the end of my life. I had a great time, even had a family and a wife. God said, What I really want to know, is what did you think I meant when I said,

'Go'?"

Matt Malyon

But store up for yourselves treasures in heaven, where moth and rust do not destroy, and where thieves do not break in and steal.
Matthew 6:20

God's unity is certainly in the midst of diversity,
but meanwhile we need a greater biblical, compassionate
strategy for releasing finance. At the same time, we need the
highest level of reality and integrity in all our fund raising.

George Verwer

But seek first his kingdom and his righteousness,
and all these things will be given to you as well.
Matthew 6:33

Moving can seem dangerous in this stranger's pilgrimage,
knowing that you can't stand still, you cross the bridge.
There's a higher place to go- beyond belief.

Bob Hartman

25

MILLION

CHILDREN

MAKE THEIR HOME

IN THE STREETS.

(100 MILLION SPEND THE DAY THERE.)

Without Holy Spirit boldness,
the world will remain unevangelized...
there can never be a substitute for the

power of the Spirit

working through willing men and women,
and that power will bring boldness.

George Verwer

"Again, the kingdom of heaven is like a merchant
looking for fine pearls. When he found one of great value,
he went away and sold everything he had and bought it."

Matthew 13:46

Matthew 16:19

I will give you the keys of
the kingdom of heaven;
whatever
you bind on earth will
be bound in heaven, and
whatever
you loose on earth will
be loosed in heaven.

There is **no limit**
to what can be accomplished if it doesn't matter who gets the credit.

Ralph Waldo Emerson

Don't allow fear of the unknown to cause you to miss out on what God wants to do through you. Worse than failure is living with the regret of never having stepped out in faith to pursue your vision.

Andy Stanley

Vision is what you will seek to achieve within the parameters of your calling. Vision is too crucial to ignore, to squander or to misunderstand.

George Barna

Ideas

not coupled with action never get bigger than the brain cells they occupy.

George Bernard Shaw

First think WOW with God for missions. The HOW will follow. Never think HOW before WOW.

Dan & Dave Davidson

With God all things are possible.

Matthew 19:26

And everyone who has left
houses OR brothers OR sisters OR
father OR mother OR children OR fields
for my sake
will receive a hundred times
as much and will inherit eternal life.

Matthew 19:29

MISSIONS IS
THE OVERFLOW OF OUR
DELIGHT IN GOD
BECAUSE MISSIONS IS THE OVERFLOW
OF GOD'S DELIGHT IN BEING GOD.

John Piper

And this gospel of the kingdom will be preached in the **whole world** as a testimony to **all nations**, and then the end will come.

Matthew 24:14

"His master replied,

'Well done,

good and faithful servant!
You have been faithful with a few things;
I will put you in charge of many things.
Come and share your master's happiness!'

Matthew 25:21

God is not looking for nibblers of the possible,
but for grabbers of the impossible.

C.T. Studd

It's so easy to lose the vision for souls...
If you have no time to drop your important job
and tell someone about Christ, then you are

too busy.

George Verwer

For I was hungry and you gave me something to eat,
I was thirsty and you gave me something to drink.
I was a stranger and you invited me in, I needed clothes
and you clothed me, I was sick and you looked after me,
I was in prison and you came to visit me...

'The King will reply, 'I tell you the truth,
whatever you did for one of the least of these
brothers of mine, you did for me.'
Matthew 25:35,40

G.O.S.P.E.L.
God Offers Sinful People Eternal Life™

Rise and shine friend, everyone you meet today is on Heaven's Most Wanted list.

Chuck Swindoll

Therefore **go** and make *disciples* of all nations, baptizing them in the name of the Father and of the Son and of the Holy Spirit, and teaching them to obey everything I have commanded you. And surely I am with you always, to the very end of the age.

Matthew 28:19,20

ome,

llow me,"

 ıs said, "and I will

ke you fishers of men."

rk 1:17

e difference between catching men

l catching fish is that you catch fish

t are alive and they die, you catch men

t are dead and bring them to life.

son Trautman

What can I do, Lord for you and your kingdom?
How can I pray every day for your Great Commission?
What can I give? How should I live reaching out to everyone?
Where can I go to let others know about your Son?

Dan Davidson

If a man does not keep
pace with his companions
perhaps it is because he hears a
different drummer.
Let him step to the music he hears
however measured and far away.

Henry David Thoreau

Life shrinks or expands in proportion to one's courage.

Anais Nin

Give me the young man who has brains
enough to make a fool of himself.

Robert Louis Stevenson

ou do not test the

resources

f God until you attempt
ie impossible.

B. Meyer

If we did all the things we were capable of
doing we would literally astonish ourselves.

Thomas Edison

Be a pioneer and open a frontier.

Cyrano De Words-u-lac

1/3 OF THE WORLD

IS UNDER THE AGE OF 15

& MOST PEOPLE MAKE
LIFE-SHAPING FAITH DECISIONS
BEFORE THE AGE OF

20

For even the Son of Man
did not come to be served, but to serve,
and to give his life as a ransom for many.
Mark 10:45

I would prefer to be in prison for two years than to do nothing for God.

Gao Feng

Everyone's life is a testimony in the making.

Dan Davidson

Failures for the believer are always temporary.
God loves you and me so much that he will
allow almost any failure if the end result
is that we become more like Jesus.

George Verwer

Mark 16:15

He said to them,

"Go into all the world *and preach the good news* to <u>all</u> creation."

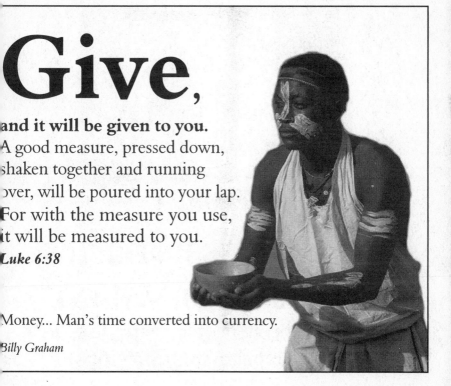

Give,

and it will be given to you.
A good measure, pressed down,
shaken together and running
over, will be poured into your lap.
For with the measure you use,
it will be measured to you.
Luke 6:38

Money... Man's time converted into currency.

Billy Graham

For out of the overflow of his heart his mouth speaks.

Luke 6:45

We are all **missionaries.**

Wherever we go,

we either bring people nearer to Christ,
or we repel them from Christ.

Eric Liddell

... If anyone would **come** after me, he must **deny** himself and **take** up his cross and **follow** me.

LUKE 9:23

So the answer to
'What's the point of mobilization?'
is to release millions of hours of prayer
and finances and workers into the harvest force...
To see churches planted, discipled, and reaching out
into their own cultures and then on into other cultures.
All in order to glorify Him together for eternity.

Bob Sjogren & Bill & Amy Stearns

...The harvest is plentiful, workers are few.
Ask the Lord of the harvest, therefore,
to send out workers
into his harvest field. - *Luke 10:2*

UNTIL CLOSING TIME,
GOD WILL ALWAYS ALLOW
DIVINE APPOINTMENTS
TO BE RESCHEDULED.
IN HEAVEN
THERE IS ONE THING
WE CAN *NEVER* DO...
WE CANNOT SHARE THE GOSPEL

Dave Davidson

In him was life, and that
life was the light of men.
John 1:4

One of the greatest ways to stay on the cutting edge
of world missions, is to be involved in evangelism yourself,
especially with people from other lands who may live right in your midst.
Beware of the struggles you will face as you launch into this: there will be
failure; there will be disappointments. But remember that disappointment in
evangelism can often be God's appointment to teach us something greater
and something better. We have to stand against the fiery dart of discouragement. I have wrestled with this all my Christian life. God's grace is sufficient. Great biblical, **mountain-moving faith**
does not happen without doubts, struggles and discouragement or
even sin. It happens in the midst of those things. When we claim
the cleansing of the precious blood of Christ, renew ourselves through
the work of the Holy Spirit and come back to the cross, He will enable
us to obey His commission to take the gospel to others.

George Verwer

HE IS NO FOOL
WHO GIVES
WHAT HE CANNOT KEEP
TO GAIN
WHAT HE CANNOT LOSE.

Jim Elliot

For God

so loved the world

that he gave his one and only Son,
that whoever believes in him
shall not perish but have eternal life.
John 3:16

AS SURELY AS

GOD LIVES,

HIS PLAN IS FOR HIS PEOPLE TO FINISH WORLD EVANGELISM

Norm Lewis

What we need are tasks in which we can see a combination of the "possible" and the "impossible". We want to be filled with faith and be realistic.

George Verwer

John 5:24 I tell you the truth,
whoever hears my word
and believes him who sent me *has eternal life*
and will not be condemned; he has crossed over from death to life

There are 130 million Muslims in India *(a minority)*

Hell: truth found too late.
Heaven: tragedy averted.

Dave Davidson

There is no higher calling or greater privilege known to man than being involved in helping fulfill the great commission.

Bill Bright

Do the thing you fear and the death of fear is certain.

Ralph Waldo Emerson

As long as it is day, we must do the work of him who sent me.

Night is coming, when no one can work.

John 9:4

It is easier

to serve God ***without a vision***, easier to work for God ***without a call***, because then you are not bothered by what God requires; *common sense* is your guide, veneered over with Christian sentiment. But if you receive a commission from Jesus Christ, the memory of what God wants will always come like a goad; and you will no longer be able to work for Him on the *common sense* basis.

Oswald Chambers

Jesus, the ultimate missionary, had a message: Repent, for the Kingdom of God is at hand. His parables were about the Kingdom. He taught people to pray, "Thy Kingdom come, Thy will be done ON EARTH as it is in heaven."

Tony Campolo

SELFISHNESS

IS NOT SIMPLY UNATTRACTIVE, IT'S

DEADLY.

Norm Lewis

MISSION OMISSION:
(8 of every 10 dollars held by Christians
are in the hands of American Christians.)

Jesus never used the word success, but he did
speak often about faithfulness.

Peter Maiden

the warped view:

**Did Jesus come to the end
of His ministry and then at the last
moment put His hand to His head and say,**

"Listen, men, I forgot to tell you something!

Boy, is this embarrassing.

I'm about to go to be with the Father... You also need to know that
you're supposed to go and reach the nations. I know you've got
lots
of questions, but I've got to go back to the Father, so I'll send the
Holy Spirit to teach you all you're supposed to know about this."
And that was the Great Commission.

Bob Sjogren, Bill & Amy Stearns

I have set you an example that you
should do as I have done for you.

John 13:15

Could a *mariner* sit idle
If he heard the drowning cry?

Could a *doctor* sit in comfort
And just let his patients die?

Could a *fireman* sit idle,
Let men burn and give no hand?

Can **you** sit at ease in Zion
With unreached peoples damned?

Leonard Ravenhill

God will always reveal His will to one who is willing to do it.

Hilys Jasper

A c t s   1 : 8

But you will receive power

when the Holy Spirit comes on you;

and you will be my witnesses

in Jerusalem, and in all Judea and Samaria, and

to the ends of the earth.

For we cannot help speaking about what we have seen and heard.
Acts 4:20

Somewhere, some way, somehow,
opportunities await for you right now.

Dave Davidson

'Leave your country
and your people,' God said,
'and go to the land I will show you.
Acts 7:3

God can use anyone who loves Jesus.

George Verwer

The Great Commission calls us to not only send money, but ourselves. Just as the Father sent the Son to become man and dwell among us, Jesus sends us into the world to personally identify with those whom we would reach. This will not always be the most economical solution, but it will be the greatest demonstration of love: We cared enough to surrender our comfort and way of life to share God's love with others.

Craig Ott

The purpose of life is a life of purpose.

Robert Byrne

It takes a heart of a hero to lay down your life.

Brian Wooten

The bible is a missionary book. Jesus Christ
is the Father's missionary to a lost world.

Harold Lindsell

The Spirit of Christ is the spirit of missions
and the nearer we get to him the more
intensely missionary we must become.

Henry Martyn

e cannot expect God to pour out His blessing unless we are
illing to become involved in some kind of redemptive service.
'hatever form our service might take, at its heart will be world
angelism-bringing all nations by all means to know Christ.

bert Coleman

He commanded us to preach to the people and to testify...

Acts 10:42

We all had an unimaginable pain
in our hearts thinking that we had
not done our utmost for the Highest,
for the One who has given life
for us on the Cross.

Richard Wurmbrand

So after they had fasted and prayed,
they placed their hands on them and

sent them off.

Acts 13:3

A feasible strategy to reaching the unreached is
each church simply sending two mature and gifted
Christians to the mission field like in Acts 13.
The field will be blessed, while room for
new leaders is made locally.

George Verwer

I believe

encouraging
workers to go
overseas will
strengthen
Christian
ministry
in the west.
Acts 13 should
revolutionize
the church.

George Verwer

However, I consider my life worth nothing to me, if only **I may finish the race** and complete the task the Lord Jesus has given me— the task of testifying to the gospel of God's grace.

Acts 20:24

Behind-the-lines
missionaries who finance
the spread of the gospel are the most
critically needed people in the world today.

Tragically,

those who are called and trained can't
find enough financing to get to the field.
They end up doing something other than what
God has called them to do, and it's not their
fault. Their failure is the failure of behind-
the-lines missionaries to do our part.

Woodrow Kroll

Anyone can live for Jesus because it is He who lives in us.

George Verwer

WORLDWIDE THERE ARE OVER
20 MILLION **REFUGEES**

& ALMOST ANOTHER 20 MILLION PEOPLE
DISPLACED WITHIN THEIR OWN COUNTRIES.

Boldly and without hindrance he preached the kingdom of God and taught about the Lord Jesus Christ.

Acts 28:31

I am *not*

ashamed

of the gospel,

because it is the power of God
for the salvation of everyone who believes:
first for the Jew, then for the Gentile.

Romans 1:16

Our God of grace ofte
gives us a second chanc
but there is *no* second chanc
to **harvest a ripe crop**

Kurt von Schleic

For since the creation of the world God
invisible qualities—his eternal power an
divine nature—have been clearly see
being understood from what has bee
made, so that men are without excus
Romans 1:2

Prayer moves the har
that moves the worl

John Aikman Wal

God always gives his best to those

who leave the choice with Him.

Jim Elliot

Now if we are children, then we are heirs, heirs of God
and co-heirs with Christ, if indeed we share in his sufferings
in order that we may also share in his glory.

Romans 8:17

I have always envied those Christians who were martyred for Christ Jesus
our Lord. What a privilege to live for our Lord and to die for Him as well.
I am filled to overflowing with joy; I am not only satisfied to be in prison. . .
But am ready to give my life for the sake of Jesus Christ.

Mehdi Dibaj

Prayer is at the heart of the action and a worldwide prayer movement must run parallel with any kind of worldwide mission movement.

George Verwer

I consider that our present sufferings are not worth comparing with the glory that will be revealed in us.

Romans 8:18

THE BIBLE SEEMS ADAMANT TO WARN US, TO ADVISE US & TELL US NOT TO ACCUMULATE, TO COLLECT & STORE UP MORE AND MORE THINGS, BUT TO GIVE MORE AND BE DEPRIVED

IF LOVE CALLED FOR IT.

John Piper

What would happen to this world if more evangelical Christians were to realize that God blessed them with money in order to make them a blessing, not to pamper them.

Ralph Winter

JESUS SAID, **"FOLLOW ME"** <u>HE DID NOT SAY</u>...

"HAVE GREAT DOCTRINE."
"BUY STUFF AND CHANGE CHANNELS."
"IMPROVE YOUR CAREER."
"IMAGE IS EVERYTHING."
"SIMMER DOWN NOW!"

Dave Davidson

There are about 12,000

unreached

people groups in the world today.
4,000 Muslim, 3,000 Tribal, 2,000 Hindu,
1,000 Chinese & 1,000 other groups

How, then, **can they call**
on the one they have not believed in?
And **how can they believe**
in the one of whom they have not heard?
And **how can they hear** without
someone preaching to them?
Romans 10:13

Most Christians want all of the privileges
and none of the responsibilities.

George Verwer

Hungry,

hurting, native missionaries are waiting to go on to the next village with the gospel, but they need your prayer and financial support.

K. P. Yohannan

And **how** can they **preach** unless they are sent? As it is written, "How beautiful are the feet of those who bring good news!"
Romans 10:14,15

Make it essential to pursue potential.

Cyrano De Words-u-lac

We seem to have a strange idea of Christian service.
We will buy books, travel miles to hear a speaker on
blessings, pay large sums to hear a group singing the latest
Christian songs- but we forget that we are soldiers.

George Verwer

If it's God's will, it's God's bill...
How would you know if you only stand still?

Dave Davidson

Therefore, I urge you, brothers, in view of God's mercy,
to offer your bodies as living sacrifices,
holy and pleasing to God—this is your spiritual act of worship.

Romans 12:1
It's easier to steer a moving car than a parked one.

George Sweeting

If **not** us, who?
If **not** now, when?
How about *YOU*?

I'm a fanatic, if you like, but only because I believe so
strongly that nothing counts except knowing your sins have
been forgiven by the blood of Jesus. We've only got this
short life to get others to know the same truth.

Dr. Helen Roseveare

Do not conform any longer to the pattern of this world,
but be transformed by the renewing of your mind.
Then you will be able to test and approve what
God's will is—his good, pleasing and perfect will.

Romans 12:2

The hour has come for you to

wake up

from your slumber,

because our salvation is nearer
now than when we first believed.
Romans 13:11

We are not called to be the honey of the world
but the salt of the earth. Salt stings on an open
wound, but it also saves one from gangrene.

Donald Bloesch

I will place no value on

a n y t h i n g

I have or may posses except
in relation to the kingdom of Christ.
If anything will advance the interests
of that kingdom, it shall be given or
kept only as by giving or keeping it
I may advance the glory of Him
to whom I owe all my hopes
for time and eternity.

David Livingston

TELL THE STORY

I see a lady with her life gone bad her whole belongings in
her bag I see a child where it all began and if she knew the
she could mend

Tell the story sing it out loud and clear
Tell the story for the world to hear
Tell the story for the child in man
Tell the story you know you've
got to got to tell the story

I see a soldier who stood straight and tall
but now held captive by his past the war is raging
still inside his mind without foundations
it can't last my friend, it can't last

Out on the corner by a dim red glow you ask a lady does sh
know she sez she knows it, but she can't conceive how Go
could help her believe you've got to help her believe
Robert Rottet - listen to the song at PoetTree.com

It has always been my

ambition

to preach the gospel

where Christ was not known...

Romans 15:20

For the message of the cross is

foolishness

to those who are

perishing,

but to us who are being saved

it is the power of God.

1 Corinthians 1:18

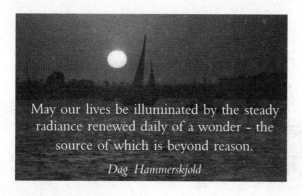

May our lives be illuminated by the steady
radiance renewed daily of a wonder - the
source of which is beyond reason.

Dag Hammerskjold

We need a constant work of the Holy Spirit.
I often tell the story about D. L. Moody who would
emphasize the need to be filled with the Spirit again
and again. One day when asked, "Mr. Moody why
do you keep saying we have to be filled again
and again?" he replied, "because I leak".

Thank God for free refills.

George Verwer

I planted the seed, Apollos watered it,

but God made it grow.

The man who plants and the man who waters have

one purpose,

and each will be rewarded according to his own labor.

1 Corinthians 3:6,8

Before we can blanket the world with the Gospel,
we must blanket the church and God's people with
the biblical vision and reality of what this is all about.

George Verwer

I will belong to the road, sharing the suffering of my people, eating with
those who will give me shelter, and telling all men of the love of God.

Sadu Sundar Singh

You are not your own;
you were bought with a price.
Therefore honor God with your body.

1 Corinthians 6:19,20

My brothers and sisters, we have been bought with a price: the blood of our holy Creator God of the universe. We are called by God to maintain our first love, to obey His command to love others, and to tell others how much He loves and cares for them. The God-man, Jesus of Nazareth, has commissioned us to help take His gospel to the ends of the Earth. Let us commit ourselves to help fulfill the Great Commission…

Bill Bright

Woe to me if I do not preach the gospel!

1 Corinthians 9:16

My life is full of unanswered prayer.
Not even 50 percent of my prayers have
been answered over the years, not yet at least.

I refuse to be
discouraged by this.

George Verwer

To the *weak* I became *weak,* to win the *weak*.
I have become all things to all men
so that by all possible means I might save some.

1 Corinthians 9:22

Don't make excuses with
"if only" and "what if".

Cyrano De Words-u-lac

If you live for having it all
you'll never have enough.

Joe Dominguez & Vicki Robin

I do all this for the
sake of the gospel,
that I may share in its blessings.
1 Corinthians 9:23

**If two roads from one unraveled,
take the one less traveled.**

Cyrano De Words-u-lac

Always eternally invest
in what will stand the test.

Cyrano De Words-u-lac

God won't always do **what
<u>we</u> say *God* should** do;
But *God* <u>will</u> always do
e x a c t l y
what *God* says *HE* <u>will</u> do.

Bill & Amy Stearns

For we are to God the aroma of Christ
among those who are being saved
and those whoare perishing.
2 Corinthians 2:15

Therefore, since we
have such a hope,
we are very

bold

2 Corinthians 3:12

2 Corinthians 4:16-18

Therefore we
do not lose heart.

Though outwardly we are wasting
away, yet inwardly we are being renewed
day by day. For our light and momentary
troubles are achieving for us an eternal
glory that far outweighs them all.
So we fix our eyes not on what
is seen, but on what is unseen.

For what is seen
is temporary, but

what is unseen is
eternal.

Sometimes I've
believed as many as six
impossible things before
breakfast.

Lewis Carroll

One doesn't discover new lands
without consenting to lose sight
of the shore for a very long time.

Andre Gide

What we need is more people
who specialize in the impossible.

Theodore Roethke

You can give without loving,
but you cannot love without giving.

Amy Carmichael

I am looking for a lot of men who have an infinite
capacity to not know what can't be done.

Henry Ford

Please promise to pray for me when I stop praying for others.

Dan Davidson

he **greatest mystery** is *why* those who

e charged with rescuing the lost have

ent two thousand years doing other things, good

ings, perhaps, but have failed to send and

e sent until all have heard the liberating word of

fe in Christ Jesus.

Robertson McQuilkin

We live by faith, not by sight.

2 Corinthians 5:7

God is seeking men and women of reckless faith today... To be reckless in your faith does not mean to be unthinking, but the reverse - concentrated, single-minded in your concern that God should be glorified and souls won.

George Verwer

The problem with problems is they're rarely seen as the opportunities God intends for us.

Dave Davidson

If your god is so great, why can't he speak my language?

Cakchiquel man asking Cameron Townsend

For Christ's love compels us,

because we are convinced that one died for all, and therefore all died.

2 Corinthians 5:14

We make a living by what we get, but we make a life by what we give.

Winston Churchill

Christianity in the West today says we must have a bigger church and a bigger car and a better suit. Once Christians fall out of love with that and in love with Jesus, I won't need to talk mission; they will become missionaries because they love Him.

Dr. Helen Roseveare

Education

is not the whole answer,
but it is a vital part of the answer.
Believers everywhere need to be
taught the basics of evangelism
and world missions. They need
to know what the Bible says.
They need to know something
of what has been done, and
then they need to know
what needs to be done
and how vital their
part is in it all.

George Verwer

God does not
call the qualified,
but qualifies the called.

Bill Hamon

And he died for all, that those who live
should no longer live for themselves but for him
who died for them and was raised again.
2 Corinthians 5:15

**The best way to begin, the surest route to start,
is to envision the end, then proceed with the heart.**

Dave Davidson

He is omnipotent;
God is capable of doing anything.

Bill Bright

Our purpose is connected to how God sees us and how we are to see ourselves. It is vital to our sense of identity that we understand our purpose in life.

Josh McDowell

When we see the great magnitude of his sacrifice for us, when we realize the great need of many to hear the message, and when we envision what it will be like one day to stand before him as his bride, then we will be truly inspired and empowered to serve in his redeeming mission.

John M. Criswell

We are therefore Christ's

ambassadors,

as though God were making his appeal through us.
We implore you on Christ's behalf:
Be reconciled to God.

2 Corinthians 5:20

Whether you're the hands, feet or belly button
discover your gifts in the body of Christ and move.

Dan Davidson

We are not just engaged in some vague philanthropic exercise.
We are dealing with life and death. And we had better get
on with this business of proclaiming the Gospel.

Chuck Colson

Each man should give what he has
decided in his heart to give, not reluctantly
or under compulsion, for God loves a

cheerful giver.

2 Corinthians 9:7

A man's treatment of money is the most decisive test
of his character - how he makes it and spends it.

James Moffat

What represents the "widow's mite" in your life?
Are you willing to give it away?

Dan Davidson

And **God is able** to make all grace <u>abound</u> to you, so that in **all** things at **all** times, having **all** *that you need*, you will <u>abound</u> in **every** good work.

2 Corinthians 9:8

All that we have, all that we do,
all that we are, Lord we give to you.

Dan Davidson

If you are discouraged by your

"humanness"

in the face of the Great Commission, overwhelmed and paralyzed by the size of the challenge then consider for a moment Paul's approach to his weakness expressed in 2 Corinthians 12:8-10. We tend to forget that however filled with the Spirit we may be, there is still the human factor. We are ordinary people who struggle, make mistakes and have weaknesses. I have become more and more convinced that God fills and uses different types of people, many of whom may not look very promising by normal standards.

George Verwer

Time flies
hen you haven't begun.

h Myrrh

ho in heaven will thank
od for *you* playing a part
their salvation?

e Davidson

ffering did not diminish my
h, but only intensified my
ationship with Jesus.

hong Miao

**No one really knows why they're
alive until they know what they'd die for.**

Martin Luther King Jr.

Am I trying to win the approval of men, or of God?
Or am I trying to please men? If I were still trying
to please men, I would not be a servant of Christ.

Galatians 1:10

I have been crucified with Christ and I no longer
live, but Christ lives in me. The life I live in the
body, I live by faith in the Son of God, who
loved me and gave himself up for me.

Galatians 2:20

It costs
more to
do
nothing.

Dave Davidson

Let us not become
weary in doing good, for at
the proper time we will reap a
harvest if we do not give up.
Galatians 6:9

I pray also that the eyes of your heart
may be enlightened in order that you may

know the hope to
which he has called you,

the riches of his glorious inheritance in the saints.

Ephesians 1:18

Make sure Jesus Christ is Lord of your life.

George Verwer

There is no magic in small plans. When I consider my ministry,
I think of the world. Anything less than that would not be
worthy of Christ, nor of His will for my life.

Henrietta Mears

For we are God's workmanship,

created in Christ Jesus **to do** good works, which God prepared in advance for us **to do**.

Ephesians 2:10

My Lord was pleased to die for my sins; why should I not be glad to give up my poor life out of love for Him.

Girolamo Savanarola

I feel very happy since the Lord called me to step out in faith, and I obeyed. The Lord is our inexhaustible treasure.

Pandita Ramabai

..And I pray that you,
being rooted and established in love,
may have power, together with all the saints,
to grasp how wide and long and high and deep is the love
of Christ, and to know this love that surpasses knowledge
that you may be filled to the measure of all the fullness of God.
Now to him who is able to do immeasurably more than all we ask
or imagine, according to his power that is at work within us, to him
be glory in the church and in Christ Jesus throughout all generations,
for ever and ever! Amen.

Ephesians 3:17-21

If God can do more than we ask or imagine, why not ask for more imagination.

Dave Davidson

Because of Jesus, it is not difficult to be a Christian,
although there are many oppressions.

Perus Kristian

WAR

we're in one (just a little reminder)

**Finally be strong in the Lord
and in his mighty power.**

Ephesians 6:10

If you have a vision to reach your neighborhood,
your town, or even all of America, Rejoice!
You're seeing God's heart for 5% of the world's population...

S t a n d U p

with an expanded vision of God's whole heart for the uttermost
parts of the world, and get to know the rest of your God.

Bob Sjogren

I eagerly expect and hope that I will in no way be ashamed,
but will have sufficient courage so that now as always Christ
will be exalted in my body, whether by life or by death.
Philippians 1:20

For to me,
to live is Christ
and to die is gain.

Philippians 1:21

God expects us to do what is in our power to do, enabled by
His grace. Anything that is possible for us to do is required.

Ralph Winter

What could be worse than being born without sight?
Being born with sight and no vision.

Helen Keller

When my days are wrinkled, time running
short, never want to say, **"What have I done?"**
So I transport my life, view it from the grave,
each minute spent is one we cannot save.

Matt Malyon

...But one thing I do: Forgetting what is behind and straining
toward what is ahead, I press on toward the goal to win the prize
for which God has called me heavenward in Christ Jesus.

Philippians 3:13-14

Even the devil regards mission work as a great idea.
He has young people in false cults serving mandatory
two-year terms. Will you not commit even more to Jesus?

Dave Davidson

"... it all comes down
to the discipline of

daring,

of being willing to take risks for
God. This is what the life of faith is,
by definition... We must be willing as
Caleb to dare, to gamble and trust."

George Verwer

Dare to dream to the extreme.

Cyrano De Words-u-lac

But our citizenship is in

heaven...

And we eagrly await a Savior fro
there, the Lord Jesus Chr

Philippians

No Reserve.
No Retreat.
No Regrets.

William Borden

I am not saying this because I am in need, for I have learned to be content whatever the circumstances. I know what it is to be in need, and I know what it is to have plenty. I have learned the secret of being content in any and every situation, whether well fed or hungry, whether living in plenty or in want.

I can do everything
through him who gives me strength.
Philippians 4:11-13

YOU WOULD
BELIEVE

IN PIONEER MISSIONS
IF <u>YOUR</u> FAMILY WERE A
PART OF AN UNEVANGELIZED
PEOPLE GROUP

Norm Lewis

All over the world this gospel is bearing fruit and growing...
Colossians 1:6

I have become its servant by the commission God gave me
to present to you the word of God in its fullness—the mystery
that has been kept hidden for ages and generations,
but is now disclosed to the saints.

Colossians 1: 25, 26

Whether you make shoes or microchips, God can use you.

George Verwer

Christ sent me to preach the gospel and He will look after the results.

Mary Slessor

And whatever you do, whether in word or deed,
do it all in the name of the Lord Jesus, giving
thanks to God the Father through him.

Colossians 3:17

Our hour is unprecedented, our jungle is

uncharted,

our opportunities are unmatched.

A. T. Pierson

Devote yourselves to prayer, being watchful and thankful.

Colossians 4:2

Without faith and love your Christianity
will be a hollow thing, no matter what
its intellectual credibility.

George Verwer

God has prepared
the **whole world**
for the gospel and the gospel
for the **whole world**.

Don Richardson

I love to live on the brink of eternity.

David Brainerd

We loved you so much that we were delighted to share
with you not only the gospel of God but our lives
as well, because you had become so dear to us.
1 Thessalonians 2:8

If Jesus Christ be God
and died for me,
then *no sacrifice* can
be too great for me
to make for Him.

C. T. Studd

He called you to this through our
gospel, that you might share in the
glory of our Lord Jesus Christ.

2 Thessalonians 2:14

The Great Commission
is more than a call for you and me to
leave where we are and go somewhere else.
There is of course a great need for people to go but,
there is a greater need for each of us to take up our own

responsibility

for the church's response to the Great Commission;
to be personally involved in it whatever our
particular role may be.

George Verwer

Our God is a Missionary God.

John Stott

as of now
1.8 BILLION
PEOPLE
HAVE LITTLE CHANCE OF
HEARING THE GOSPEL.

People seem to not realize that their opinion
of the world is also a confession of character.

Ralph Waldo Emerson

Mission gives your life purpose. Vision gives your
life direction. Values give you character.

George Barna

Prayer is where the **action** is,

supporting

and sustaining those on the fields...

Neal Pirolo

Wherever you are, be all there.
Live life to the hilt every situation you
believe to be the will of God.

Jim Elliot

I urge, then, first of all, that requests,
prayers, intercession and thanksgiving
be made for everyone—

1 Timothy 2:1

Sometimes giving anonymously is as hard as taking in film and never getting to see the photos.

Hugh Myrrh

Consistent giving strengthens the heart, tones the wallet and exercises your faith.

Dave Davidson

You do have to be aware of the needs and opportunities throughout the world as you consider your own future. This is a challenge to consider seriously your own personal response to the command and the promise of Jesus in the Great Commission. You are called to make a decision.

George Verwer

Through prayer

any of us can directly

love the unreached,

even to the ends of the earth.

As far as God can go,
prayer can go.

David Bryant

Prayer keeps us looking.
Prayer keeps the burden fresh.
It keeps our eyes and hearts in an

expectant mode.

Prayer doesn't force God's hand.
But it keeps us on the lookout for his

intervention.

Andy Stanley

For there is one God and one mediator between
God and men, the man Christ Jesus...
1 Timothy 2:5

It's like you're going to the **greatest party** ever and get to invite anyone you want.

Dave Davidson

I have but one candle of life to burn, and would rather burn it out where people are dying in darkness than in a land which is flooded with lights.
anonymous missionary

Watch your life and doctrine closely. Persevere in them, because if you do, you will save both yourself and your hearers.
1 Timothy 4:16

Fight the good fight of the faith.

Take hold of the eternal life to which you were called...

1 Timothy 6:12

Command those who are rich in this present world not to be arrogant nor to put their hope in wealth, which is so uncertain, but to put their hope in God, who richly provides us with everything for our enjoyment. Command them to do good, to be rich in good deeds, and to be generous and willing to share.

1 Timothy 6:17,18

It's not what I'm going to do for You (God), but rather what You're going to do through me.

Luis Palau

IF YOU SEE **10** MEN TRYING TO LIFT A LOG, **9** OF THEM ON THE LIGHT END AND **1** ON THE HEAVY END, WHERE WILL <u>YOU</u> STEP IN TO HELP?

William Borden

Endure hardship with us like a good soldier of Christ Jesus.

2 Timothy 2:3

Therefore
I endure everything
for the **sake of the elect**,

that they too may obtain the salvation that is
in Christ Jesus, with eternal glory.
2 Timothy 2:10

My greatest help in Christ is that moment by
moment I can pass my distress over to him.

George Verwer

IN **TURKEY**

THE IS ONLY **1**

CHRISTIAN FOR EVERY

160,000 PEOPLE

Break my heart

with the things that break the heart of God.

Bob Pierce

Better a slap in the face now than tears of regret later.

Dave Davidson

The mission of the church is missions.

Sidney Correll

FOR THE REST OF MY DAYS

For the rest of my days and in all of my ways.
Lord I will live my life with no regret. Work a little longer. Pray a little
stronger. Laugh a little louder. Sleep a little shorter. Then with these
things we've got the King who will work right by our side.

Robert Rottet, listen to the song at PoetTree.com

Do your best

to present yourself to God as one approved,
a workman who does not need to be ashamed
and who correctly handles the word of truth.

2 Timothy 2:15

Once we begin to really obey
God and hence see fruit in our lives,
then we gain a greater assurance.

George Verwer

I intend to keep on going, preaching the gospel,
writing the gospel as long as I have any breath.
I hope my last word as I am dying ... will be Jesus.

Billy Graham

Evangelism should be as natural as breathing.

Bill Hybels

Preach the word

be prepared in season and out of season;
correct, rebuke and encourage—with
great patience and careful instruction.

2 Timothy 4:2

Wisdom and discernment are essential as we consider
taking action on missions. A. W. Tozer said that the greatest
gift we need in the church today is the gift of discernment.
This sometimes comes like a supernatural lightning bolt,
but more often as we become saturated with scripture.

George Verwer

God is most glorified when we are satisfied in Him.

John Piper

"When you can put your *church* on the back of a *camel*, then I will believe *Christianity* is for us."

a Somali camel herder

Many put missions' call on hold,
yet need no call for a telemarketing job.

John Donut

Forsake your wimp factor, take a step and be proactive

George Verwer

If we have a further end in view, we do not pay
sufficient attention to the immediate present;
if we realize that obedience is the end, then
each moment as it comes is precious.

Oswald Chambers

I pray that you may be

active

in sharing your faith,
so that you will have a full understanding
of every good thing we have in Christ.

Philemon 1:6

C.S. Lewis said that we have the tendency to think, but not to act
and to feel, but not to act. If we go on feeling and thinking,
but not acting, then one day we will be unable to act.

George Verwer

Let us hold
unswervingly
to the hope we profess,
for he who promised is faithful.

Hebrews 10:23

I have resolved that the Lord Jesus Christ shall have all of me.

Billy Graham

Goals create priorities, determine decisions, dictate companions, and predict choices.

Myles Munroe

Shine.

ke 'em wonder what you've got
e 'em wish that they were not
he outside looking bored.
ne. Let it shine before all men.
'em see good works and then
em glorify the Lord.

Taylor

You are here to be a light to your world.
You are a city on a hill.
You are a beacon in this dark night.

Andy Stanley

Generosity

increases our joy because it frees us. It releases us from the grip of money because we have the courage to give it away. In days of economic uncertainty, many spend precious emotional energy worrying about the future. They fear either not getting what they want or losing what they have. Generosity puts our lives in a wider arena. We take our eyes off ourselves and realize that God is our provider, and He will take care of us.

Paul Borthwick

What we taste, touch and tabulate can never be our satisfaction.

Lloyd J. Ogilvi

If you wanted
to please your
FATHER

you would do something
which is close to His heart.
With God it's the same.

Dave Davidson

And without faith
it is impossible
to please God...

Hebrews 11:6

Sure it seems like a mountain now, but half way up there it looks more like a hill.

Dave Davidson

We proclaim to others that God is the Living God. Let us prove his livingness in the very practical realm of material things.

Watchman Nee

Therefore, since we are surrounded by such a great cloud of witnesses, let us throw off everything that hinders and the sin that so easily entangles, and let us run with perseverance the race marked out for us.

Hebrews 12:1

I have decided

to follow Jesus with my whole life,
and I understand where he's going.
...if my actions stem from a biblical
worldview... it's no longer a matter of
choosing a career or lifestyle-it's
a matter of faithfulness.

Sam Wilson & Gordon Aeschilman

Consider him who endured such opposition
from sinful men, so that you will not
grow weary and lose heart.
Hebrews 12:3

Have a sense of **urgency** in times of emergency.

Cyrano De Words-u-lac

Therefore, since we are receiving a kingdom that cannot be shaken, let us be thankful, and so worship God acceptably with reverence and awe...
Hebrews 12:28

The secret to falling in love with Jesus forever is to honor Him fearfully, keeping His promises faithfully.

Dan & Dave Davidson

ople are always blaming their

circumstances

r what they are. I don't believe in

circumstances.

The people who get on in this world are
the people who get up and look for the

circumstances

they want, and, if they can't find
them, make them.

George Bernard Shaw

Often times the best foot forward is a
swift kick in the seat of the pants.

Hugh Myrrh

All brave men were once
cowards
who just quit not asking.

Dave Davidson

One-fifth of all people are
against everything all the time.
Robert Kennedy

Don't play for safety; it's the most
dangerous thing in the world.
Hugh Walpole

The moment you alter your perception
of yourself and your future, both you
and your future begin to change.
Marilee Zdenek

View your pressures
no longer as burdens but as a
platform
for His glorious sufficiency.

Clarence W. Jones

Unless the church fulfills its responsibility to proclaim by word
and deed the Good News to the poor, the poor have no real hope.
We, the church, bear the only true gospel of hope. Only through
us can the power of Christ's love save and deliver them.

John Perkins

Consider it pure joy, my brothers, whenever you face
trials of many kinds, because you know that the
testing of your faith develops perseverance.
James 1:2,3

And the things you have heard me say in the presence of many witnesses entrust to reliable men who will also be qualified to teach others.

2 Timothy 2:2

Go over, around or through obstacles in front of you.

Cyrano De Words-u-lac

You're running a risk whenever you're not running a risk.

Dave Davidson

A missions mobilizer is a Christian who not only wants to get involved in evangelism and missions work but who wants to get other people involved as well.

George Verwer

The Holy Spirit does not wait
for all our cultural baggage to disappear
before he can use us in a powerful way.

George Verwer

Perseverance

must finish its work so that you may be
mature and complete, not lacking anything.

James 1:4

This generation of Christians is responsible
for this generation of sinners.

Keith Green

Blessed is the man
who perseveres under trial,
because when he has stood the test,
he will receive the crown of life that God
has promised to those who love him.

James 1:12

Do not merely listen to the word, and
so deceive yourselves. **Do** what it says.

James 1:22

The bottom line in mission work

is people work... loving them, serving them and helping
them become strong disciples of Jesus.

George Verwer

NO ONE WILL BE ABLE TO RISE TO THE

MAGNIFICENCE

OF THE MISSIONARY CAUSE WHO DOES NOT FEEL, KNOW, UNDERSTAND, SEEK OR HAVE THE

MAGNIFICENCE

OF JESUS CHRIST OUR LORD.

John Piper

James 4:8 says to "Come near
to God and He will come near to you."
There is no way God is going to leave you hanging.
When in doubt always give more than you first intended.
Give more of your time and resources. God will honor your faith.
If you are considering going on a short-term missions trip or two-year
commitment and you are unsure of what to do. I encourage you
to take the initiative and start taking the steps to indeed go.
Your hometown will still be there when you return.
Your girlfriend or boyfriend may not be waiting,
but that could be a blessing in disguise.
Do you have the faith in God?

Dave Davidson

Someone is waiting to meet
Jesus on the other side of your fear.

Carman

For all the words of tongues and pen
the saddest of these: It might have been...

John Greenleaf Whittier

Why you do not even know what will happen

t o m o r r o w.

What is your life? You are a mist that appears
for a little while and then vanishes.

James 4:14

Prayer

is the Christian's vital breath:
without it you can't move.

George Verwer

...The prayer of a righteous man
is powerful and effective.
James 5:16

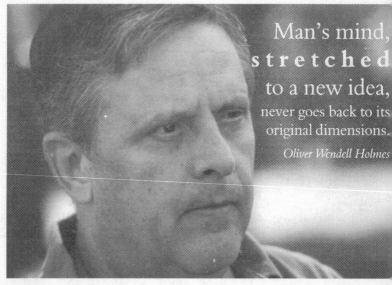

Man's mind,
stretched
to a new idea,
never goes back to its
original dimensions.

Oliver Wendell Holmes

Though you have not seen him, you love him; and even though you do not see him now, you believe in him and are filled with an inexpressible and glorious joy...

1 Peter 1:8

God can't give us happiness and peace
apart from Himself, because it is not there.
There is no such thing.

C.S. Lewis

…People overreact to extremism and end up in the deep freeze of
tradition, judgementalism, legalism, dead orthodoxy and inaction.

George Verwer

Is the salvation of souls included in your goals?

Cyrano De Words-u-lac

There are three principal postures of love:
it gives with joy, receives with appreciation,
and rebukes with humility and hope.

Albert M. Wells, Jr.

Above all,

love each other deeply,

because love covers over a multitude of sins.
1 Peter 4:8

WE ARE THE PEOPLE

We are the people the people of God, who loved us
and chose us for His own. So put on compassion.
Be gentle and meek, forgive one another like Jesus did.
We need a little more unity and some strength from above.
I can see it in you and me when we put on His love, love,
love… There's got to be more love in you, in me love…
There's got to be more love, love, love, yeah love

Robert Rottet - listen to the song at PoetTree.com

We are God's
chosen people,
not *frozen* people.
Let's pray for a defrost!

George Verwer

But you are a chosen people, a royal
priesthood, a holy nation, a people
belonging to God, that you may declare
the praises of him who called you out
of darkness into his wonderful light.
Peter 2:9

His divine power has given us

everything

we need for life and godliness
through our knowledge of him
who called us by his own glory
and goodness.
2 Peter 1:3

By taking the initiative,
we place ourselves in
God's hands as His tool
to effect change in the
lives of the lost.

Mark McCloskey

In the last analysis, it is our conception
of death which decides our answers to
all the questions that life puts to us.

Dag Hammarskjold

If at this moment you are not walking with God
and doing God's will, then you are in fact hindering

God's great program.

George Verwer

When you really know God and understand
who He is and what He has done for you,
then you can know your true identity in Christ.
Your life can change from that moment on.

Dave Davidson

Therefore, my
brothers, be all the

more eager

to make your **calling** and election
sure. For if you do these thin**gs**,

you will never fall,

and you will receive a rich welcome
into the eternal kingdom of our
Lord and Savior Jesus Christ.

2 Peter 2:10,11

Don't always go
with he tatus quo.

Cyrano De Words-u-lac

The world and its desires pass away, but the man who does the will of God lives forever. 1 John 2:17

There is no man living that cannot do more than he thinks he can. *Henry Ford*

We can choose to live more simply that others may simply live. There is enough to go around, but sharing our abundance with others will call us to cut back somewhere, to limit ourselves voluntarily, to

live a lifestyle

that reflects our knowledge of the condition of people in our world.

Paul Borthwick

There are four warnings that I often give to people who are considering missionary work. **Firstly,** your heart will be broken many times and you will face many disappointments. **Secondly,** you will face financial pressures, battles and problems and also a wide range of differences of opinion on life-style and how money should be spent. **Thirdly,** you will discover that it is sometimes relatively easy to get started on a project but unbelievably hard to keep it going and at the same time keep the loyalty of the people with whom you are working. **Fourthly,** you will discover that roots of bitterness can come in very easily in Christian work, which sometimes, due to satanic opposition, can be more difficult and complex than in secular work, especially when money and other motivating forces are absent. This is not intended to be discouraging.

There will also be, of course, blessings and joy over breakthroughs in answer to prayer. Missions work can mean a lot of fun. Many of the missionaries I know are grace-awakened people who know how to get the most out of their lives. Keeping a balance though between faith goals and unrealistic expectations is part of the process of counting the cost. *George Verwer*

Be merciful to those who doubt;
snatch others from the fire and

save them;

to others show mercy, mixed with fear...

Jude 1:22,23

ou don't ask a drowning man
he wants to be saved when
ou know he's sinking down
eneath the crashing waves.

harlie Peacock

A GLIMPSE OF HOME

When a white man and a black man stand in one church with each other in a friendship God has blessed them from above. When a landlord has a kind heart and he gives to those who need it so a family gets a house they could not afford. From the mountains to the valleys to the oceans white with foam I can feel the glimpse of home. When a prisoner gets a visitor in the name of Christ the Savior and his lonely troubled heart is not ignored. When a lawyer fights for justice in the name of God the Father and the case is a good work for the poor... Home where the lion lies with the lamb and we never more shall die. Home where my God I'll know as I am and the pain and sorrow all will fly. When the widow and the orphan find solstice and a shelter and the hungry and the hopeless have a home. When the ruler of the kingdom sends the law forth out of Zion and the nations cease to learn war anymore. From the ramparts to the vineyard where the grapes of wrath are stored. From the mountains to the valleys to the oceans white with foam I can feel the glimpse of home.

Robert Rottet - listen to the song at PoetTree.com

**You are invited to tap into the
inexhaustible resources of God.**

Andy Stanley

A Christian **missionary** is a
person whose passion is to make the Lord Jesus known to the
whole world. I believe that "being a missionary" in the truest
sense of the word is taking the Gospel **where it has never
been before**, or at least to a different culture or a different
language group. A true missionary is someone who will risk
everything for the sake of the lost of the this world.

Keith Green

Only by taking Jesus' example into every part of
our lives will we be able to win in life.

Loren Cunningham

Wait no more.

We as God's people have been very clearly commanded, commissioned, called. We are to align our lives with the objective of making followers, learners of every people including our own. In Old Testament parlance, we're to bless every people group gracing them with the privilege of joining God's family through redemption in Jesus Christ.

Bob Sjogren, Bill & Amy Stearns

1,600 new churches open worldwide each week.

In AD 100, there were 360 non-believers per true believer. Today the ratio is seven to every believer.

Approximately 70,000 people become Christians every day.

Be faithful, even to the point of death,
and I will give you the crown of life.
Revelation 2:10

What will it take for you to come to grips with
the fact that you are a part of this? It would be

ridiculous

in sports if the coach pleaded with players to
take the field and they voluntarily sat the bench.

Dave Davidson

Give up your rights and you will receive greater privileges with God.

Loren Cunningham

We need to learn how to agree to disagree and get on with
the basic living out of the Christian life, mobilizing people
for missions and presenting the gospel to the whole world.

George Verwer

Finance seems to
be the greatest obstacle...
The real obstacle is a lack of love,
faith and biblical commitment.
We can't separate what I'm saying
here from personal reformation,
reality and revival. It is a mistake to
think that the next big move is God's.
His big moves have already taken place.
The Cross; the empty tomb; and Pentecost.

NOW IT IS OUR TURN!

We need to repent and turn from all
that is hindering us from doing
God's will in our day.

George Verwer

In fact, if you don't go, you need a specific calling from God to stay home.

Has God definitely told you to **not** to "go" somewhere outside your country to preach the gospel? If He hasn't, then you'd better start praying WHERE to go, instead of IF you should go- for you're already called.

Keith Green

The devil would love to convince you that all this mission stuff isn't for you. The devil is a liar and you know it.

Dave Davidson

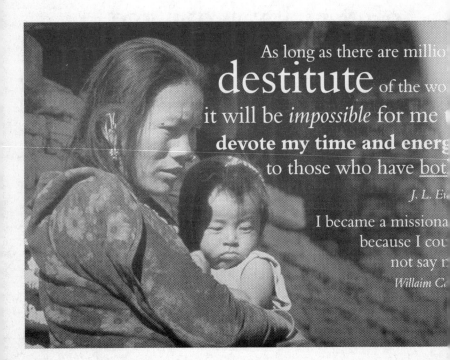

As long as there are millio[ns]

destitute of the wo[rld]

it will be *impossible* for me [to]

devote my time and energ[y]

to those who have bot[h]

J. L. Ei[...]

I became a missiona[ry]
because I cou[ld]
not say n[o]

Willaim C[...]

It can be done.
It must be done!

D. L. Moody

...every **nation**, **tribe**, **people** and **language**.
Revelation 5:9

Lord, the task is impossible for me but not for Thee.
Lead the way and I will follow. Why should I fear?
I am on a Royal Mission. I am in the service
of the King of kings.

Mary Slessor

If we
could at this time,

shrink

the Earth's population to a village of
precisely 100 people, with all exisiting human
ratios remaining the same, it would look like this:

57 Asians, 21 Europeans, 8 Africans,
14 from the Western Hemisphere
70 non-Christian, 30 Christian.
70 would be non-white, 30 white.

6 people would control 50% of the entire wealth,
all 6 of them would be from the Unitied States.

Only one would have a college education.
80 would live in substandard housing.
50 would suffer from malnutrition.
70 would be unable to read.

Net Happenings Digest

Life Tithe™

70 - 20 = 50,   10% of 50 = 5 years
3 after retirement,   2 years now

Let's estimate an average 70-year life span and consider tithing a minimum of 10% of your life to God for cross cultural mission work. Refunding the first 20 years for training, 10% of 50 years is 5 years of mission work over a 70-year life span. Consider serving 3 years after retirement, leaving a timely 2 year term right now wherever you are in life to go and serve God in missions.

Dave Davidson

If Christ could stoop so low as to visit our ... sinful world, and be moved with compassion upon the most undeserving and guilty, the most sinful and depraved ...in what better way could we demonstrate that we are partakers of His grace than by earnest endeavor to imitate His example... by laboring to promote the salvation of the most ignorant and helpless of mankind?

William Carey

Who will not fear you, O Lord, and bring glory to your name? For you alone are holy. All nations will come and worship before you...
Revelation 15:4

But if everyone exercises their rights to the exclusion of God's plans for us, a tragedy of cataclysmic proportions will occur. Millions of people will live their lives in guilt and despair and will die to face judgment for their sins eternally in hell. There are more than 2.5 billion people who've never heard the Gospel. More than 8,000 unreached people groups wait for a Christian witness.

Loren Cunningham

In tomorrow's self survey
what would you have done today?

Cyrano De Words-u-lac

Lord I know you must be coming soon
and I'll stand before this world and shout it's true.
I can't stop loving you no matter what they say.

Glenn Kaiser

"Behold, I am coming soon!
My reward is with me, and I will give to
everyone according to what he has done."
Revelation 22:12

if you come across great quotes pertaining to missions
please sumbit to: quotes@DailyMissions.com

You've read the book
  now hear the songs
    to the soundtrack of
"God's Great Ambition"
  available at **PoetTree.com**
Over 100 bible verses about world
missions as the lyrics to over 40 songs.

Also from **PoetTree.co**
The Challenge: Become famili
with the top 100 bible verses releva
to evangelism and sharing your fait
Listen to "**Here To Heaven**
a collection of 108 bible verses
42 songs in 73 minutes of musi

For a free email newsletter, bulk order info,
ministry resources and song downloads log onto

PoetTree.com

Brothers Dan and Dave Davidson share the same mission statement in the acronym T.I.M.E. - To Teach, Inspire, Motivate and Encourage. They have written 20 books together including "8 Really Relevant P.R.O.M.I.S.E.S. For Teenagers To Fall In Love With Jesus Forever."

Both brothers record verbatim scripture songs for PoetTree.com. Dan is a Chiropractor in Virginia and Dave is a photographer in Iowa. They are both inspirational speakers and missions mobilizers.

Dan and his wife Kimberly have three children.
Dave and his wife Joan have two children.

For a current list of their books and free online resources visit **DanDavidson.com** and **DaveDavidson.com** - They can be reached at Dan@DanDavidson.com and Dave@DaveDavidson.com

For more information visit
GeorgeVerwer.com
Email -
George@GeorgeVerwer.com

George Verwer is passionate about recruiting and encouraging churches to follow the Acts 13 example of sending out missionaries into the harvest fields.

eorge is the founder and International Coordinator of Operation Mobilisation, ministry of evangelism, discipleship training and church planting. He and his ife, Drena, have three adult children. They make their home in England, M's international headquarters.

eorge's mission work has taken him all over the world both in travel and rough prayer. He encourages Christians to be missions mobilizers and to live ace filled llives. As the author of several inspiring books, his most recent, Out of The Comtort Zone" is challenging people all over God's globe.

hen not using his mobile phone you can find him speaking to thousands of oung people. God uses George to stretch once preconcieved notions about issions and God's priority of reaching the world for Christ.

Meanwhile

in the last hour while reading this book over

7,000 people

who did not trust Jesus as their Savior went to hell.